The Adventures of
ARCHIBALD HIGGINS

THE BLACK HOLE

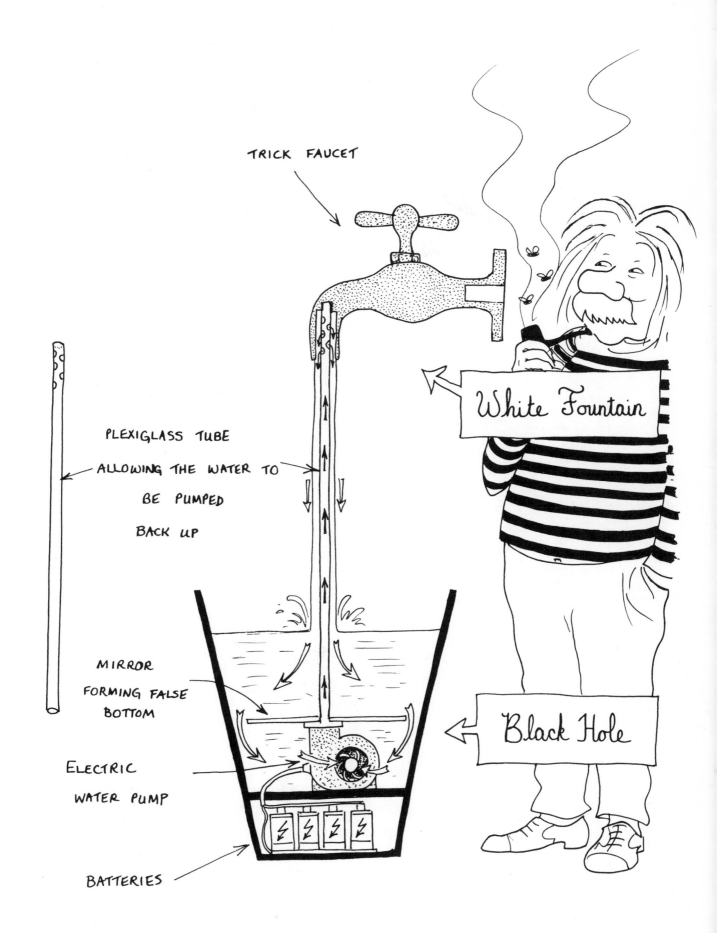

TRICK FAUCET

PLEXIGLASS TUBE
ALLOWING THE WATER TO
BE PUMPED
BACK UP

MIRROR
FORMING FALSE
BOTTOM

ELECTRIC
WATER PUMP

BATTERIES

White Fountain

Black Hole

The Adventures of
ARCHIBALD HIGGINS

The Adventures of
ARCHIBALD HIGGINS

THE BLACK HOLE

Jean-Pierre Petit

Translated by Ian Stewart

Edited by Wendy Campbell

IF THIS UNIVERSE IS THE BEST OF ALL POSSIBLE WORLDS, I'M GLAD I DON'T LIVE IN ANY OF THE OTHERS.

William Kaufmann, Inc.
Los Altos, California 94022

Originally published as *Le Trou Noir* © Belin 1981
published by Librairie Classique
Eugène Belin, Paris

Library of Congress Cataloging in Publication Data

Petit, Jean-Pierre.
  The black hole.

  (The Adventures of Archibald Higgins)
  Translation of: Le trou noir
  Summary: In his latest adventure, Archibald Higgins investigates
concepts of space and time.
    1. Space and time—Juvenile literature.
    [1. Space and time—Cartoons and comics. 2. Cartoons and
comics] I. Campbell, Wendy. II. Title. III. Series: Petit, Jean-Pierre.
Aventures d'Anselme Lanturlu. English.
QC173.59.S65P4613 1985   530.1′1   85-25609
ISBN 0-86576-069-1

ONCE MORE, ARCHIE SETS OUT TO EXPLORE THE WORLD OF MISTS.

4

A SURFACE IS A **2-DIMENSIONAL SPACE.** THAT IS, YOU NEED **TWO** NUMBERS — TWO COORDINATES — TO SPECIFY THE POSITION OF A POINT.

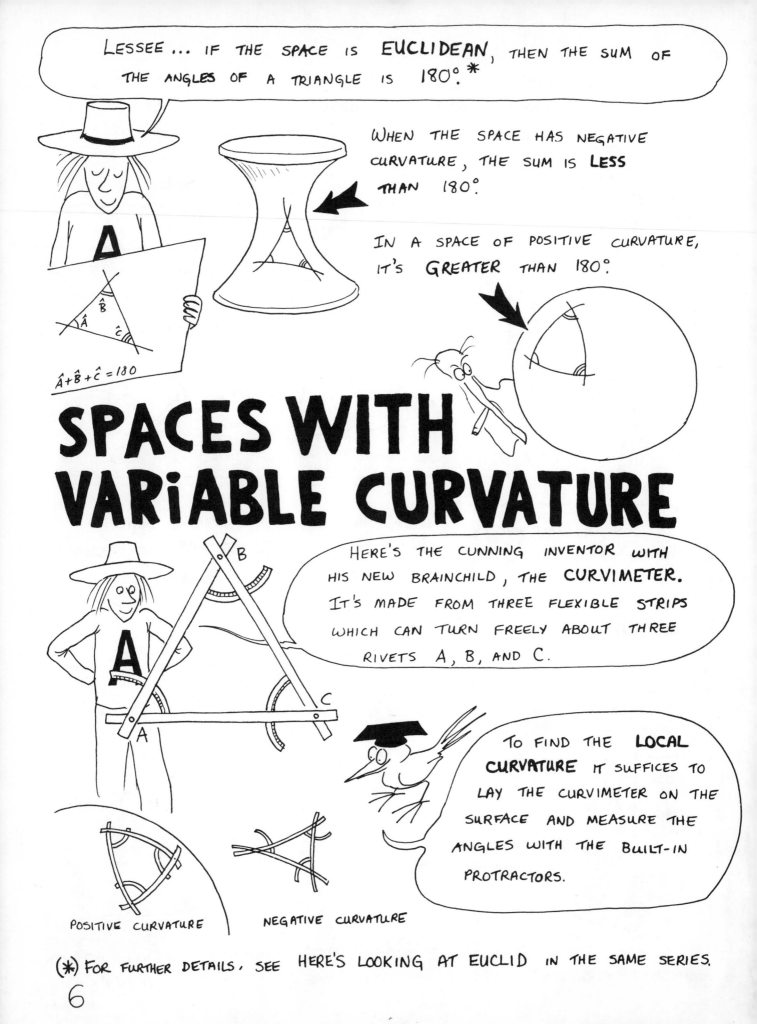

LESSEE ... IF THE SPACE IS **EUCLIDEAN**, THEN THE SUM OF THE ANGLES OF A TRIANGLE IS 180°.*

WHEN THE SPACE HAS NEGATIVE CURVATURE, THE SUM IS **LESS THAN** 180°.

IN A SPACE OF POSITIVE CURVATURE, IT'S **GREATER** THAN 180°.

$\hat{A} + \hat{B} + \hat{C} = 180$

SPACES WITH VARIABLE CURVATURE

HERE'S THE CUNNING INVENTOR WITH HIS NEW BRAINCHILD, THE **CURVIMETER**. IT'S MADE FROM THREE FLEXIBLE STRIPS WHICH CAN TURN FREELY ABOUT THREE RIVETS A, B, AND C.

TO FIND THE **LOCAL CURVATURE** IT SUFFICES TO LAY THE CURVIMETER ON THE SURFACE AND MEASURE THE ANGLES WITH THE BUILT-IN PROTRACTORS.

POSITIVE CURVATURE

NEGATIVE CURVATURE

(*) FOR FURTHER DETAILS, SEE HERE'S LOOKING AT EUCLID IN THE SAME SERIES.

6

CONICAL POINTS

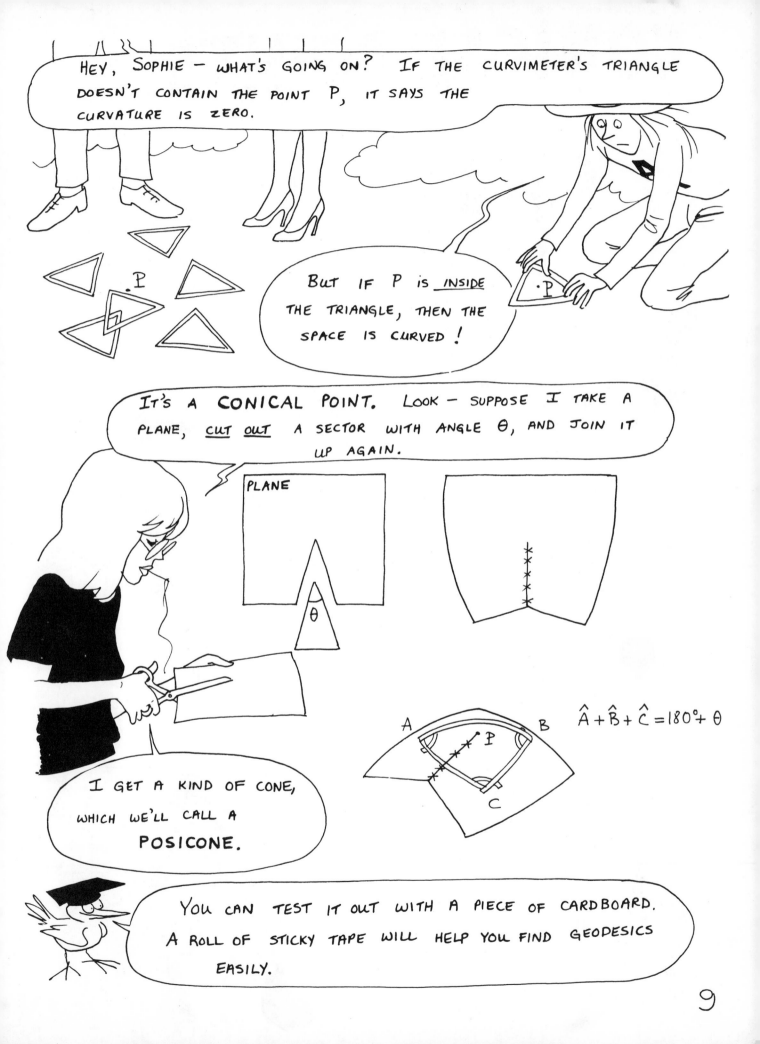

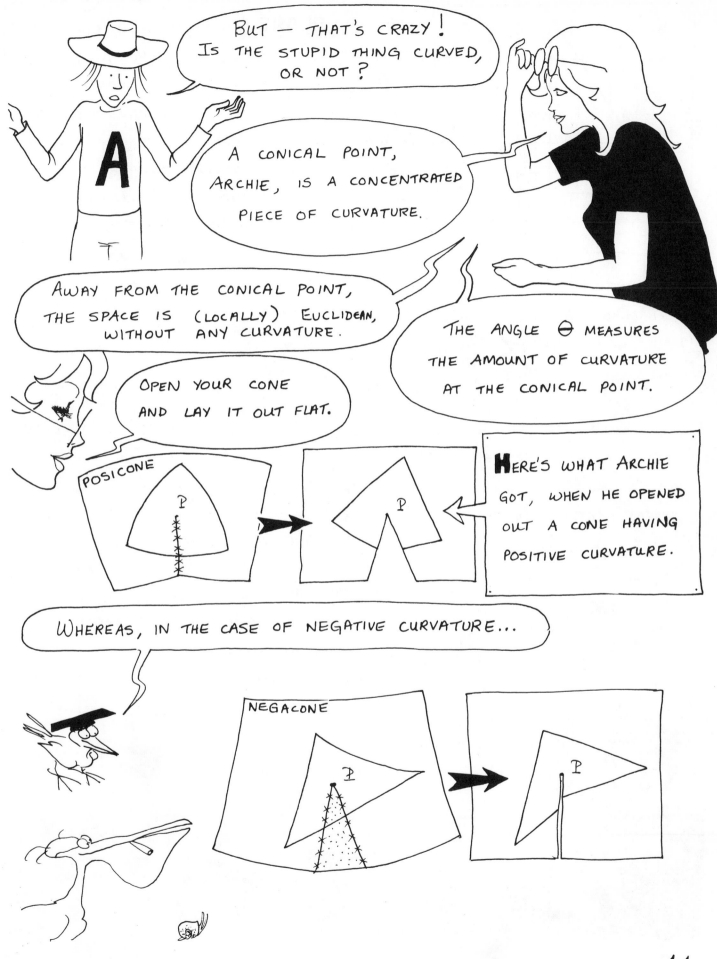

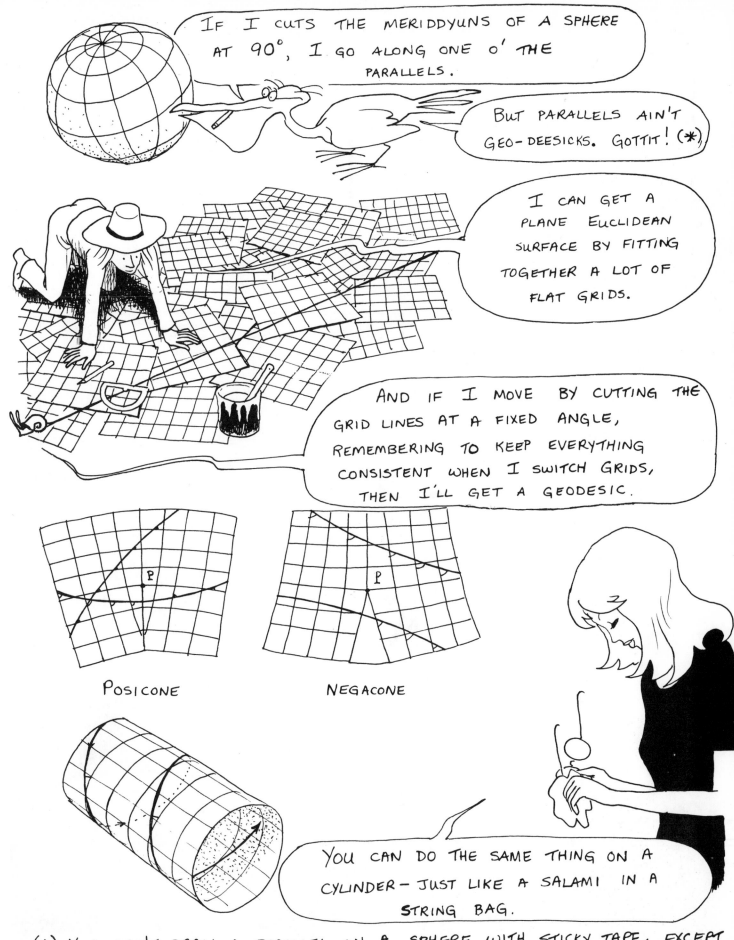

POSICONE

NEGACONE

(*) YOU CAN'T DRAW A PARALLEL ON A SPHERE WITH STICKY TAPE, EXCEPT AT THE EQUATOR. TRY IT ON A BASKETBALL.

$\hat{A} + \hat{B} + \hat{C}$
$= 90° + 90°$
$+ θ/2 + θ/2$
$= 180° + θ$

ARCHIBALD HIGGINS WILL NOW CONSTRUCT SPECIAL CONES, WHICH KEEP THE TILING REGULAR.

The Boss

THERE, I'VE CUT OUT 90°.

90°

$\hat{A} + \hat{B} + \hat{C} = 180° + 90°$
$= 270°$

ON THIS CONE YOU CAN DRAW RIGHT-ANGLED EQUILATERAL TRIANGLES.

NOW I EXCISE A SECTOR OF 180°.

180°

ON THIS CONE, YER GITS A H'ANGLE-SUM OF 360°.

WHICH IMPLIES THAT YOU CAN DRAW ON IT, USING GEODESICS, A TRIANGLE HAVING THREE ANGLES OF 120° — THAT IS, **OBTUSE**.

AND IT STILL CLOSES UP? THAT'S WEIRD.

120°

HUM...

SEEMS TER ME, TIRESIAS, THAT **YOU'RE** THE ONE WOT'S H'OBTUSE!

ME?

15

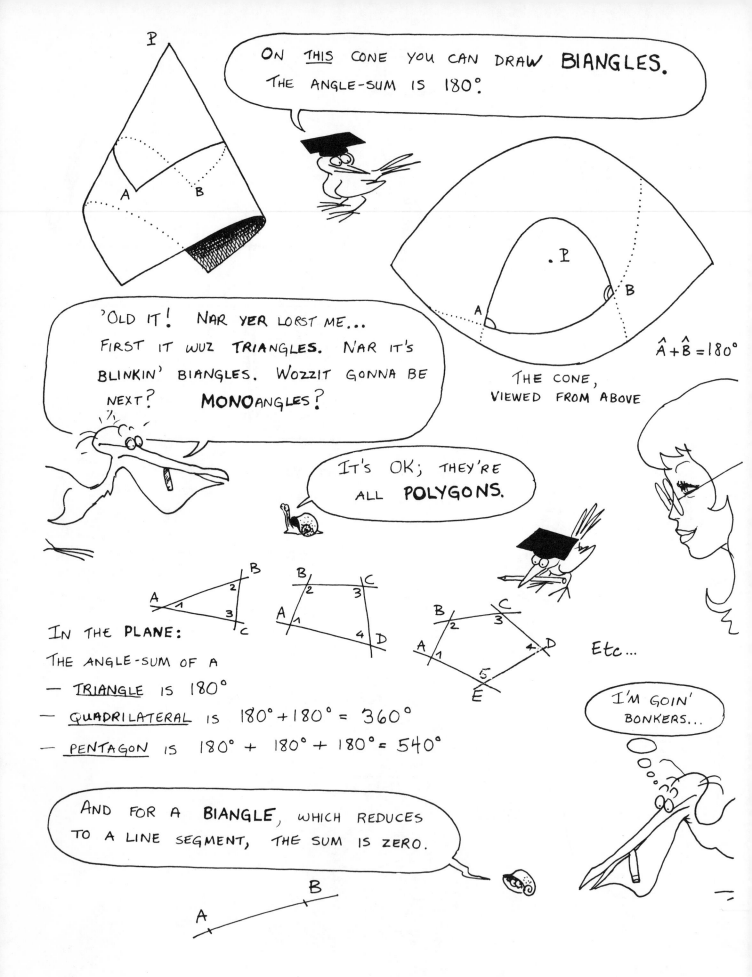

ON __THIS__ CONE YOU CAN DRAW **BIANGLES**.
THE ANGLE-SUM IS 180°.

'OLD IT! NAR YER LORST ME...
FIRST IT WUZ **TRIANGLES**. NAR IT'S
BLINKIN' BIANGLES. WOZZIT GONNA BE
NEXT? **MONO**ANGLES?

IT'S OK; THEY'RE
ALL **POLYGONS**.

$\hat{A} + \hat{B} = 180°$

THE CONE,
VIEWED FROM ABOVE

Etc...

I'M GOIN'
BONKERS...

IN THE **PLANE**:
THE ANGLE-SUM OF A
— __TRIANGLE__ IS 180°
— __QUADRILATERAL__ IS 180° + 180° = 360°
— __PENTAGON__ IS 180° + 180° + 180° = 540°

AND FOR A **BIANGLE**, WHICH REDUCES
TO A LINE SEGMENT, THE SUM IS ZERO.

16

POLES

NOW YOU SEE THE POINT OF MY REMARK.

ARE YOU TRYIN' TER NEEDLE ME?

OH 'ECK...

ANOTHER WAY TO PRODUCE THE TILINGS THAT ARCHIE GOT IS TO STRETCH SOME FABRIC.

REMOVING ALMOST ALL OF THE PLANE AND APPLYING THIS PROCEDURE IN REVERSE, YOU GET THIS: A PATTERN LIKE MERIDIANS AND PARALLELS...

... AT A POLE.

A POLE IS WHAT'S LEFT WHEN YOU TAKE EVERYTHING ELSE AWAY. JUST A CONCENTRATED CURVATURE OF 360°. OF COURSE, THE EARTH'S POLES AREN'T LIKE THAT, BECAUSE YOU DON'T HAVE TO STRETCH THE SURFACE TO SEE THE PATTERN.

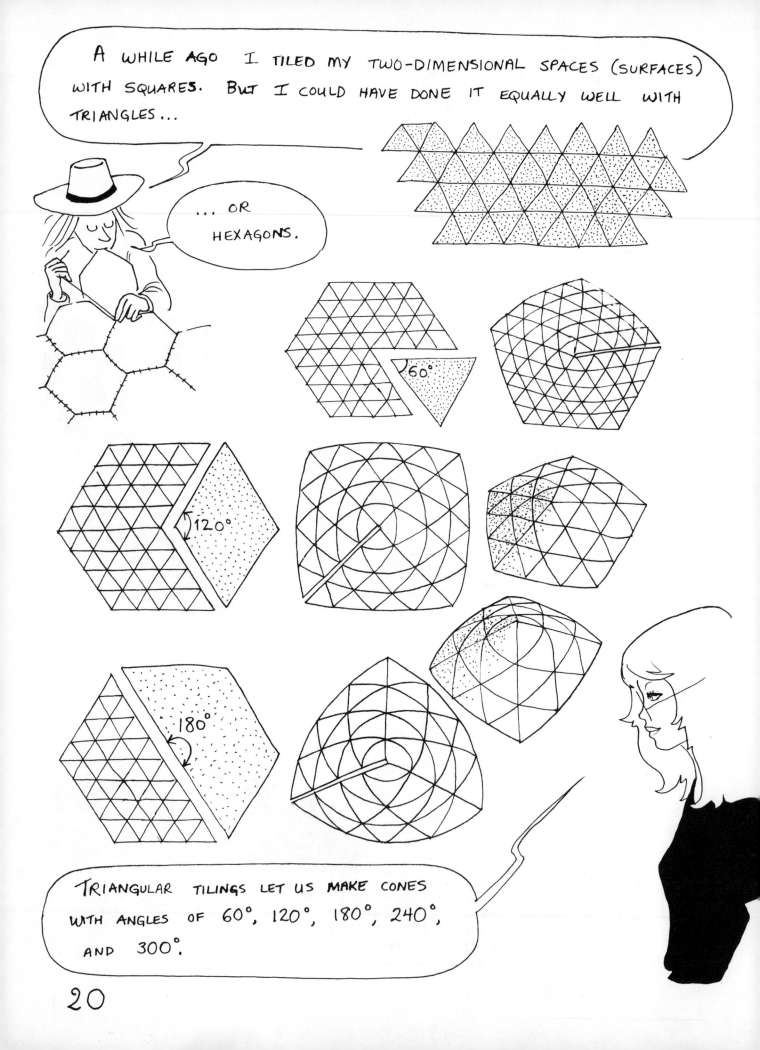

A WHILE AGO I TILED MY TWO-DIMENSIONAL SPACES (SURFACES) WITH SQUARES. BUT I COULD HAVE DONE IT EQUALLY WELL WITH TRIANGLES...

... OR HEXAGONS.

60°

120°

180°

TRIANGULAR TILINGS LET US MAKE CONES WITH ANGLES OF 60°, 120°, 180°, 240°, AND 300°.

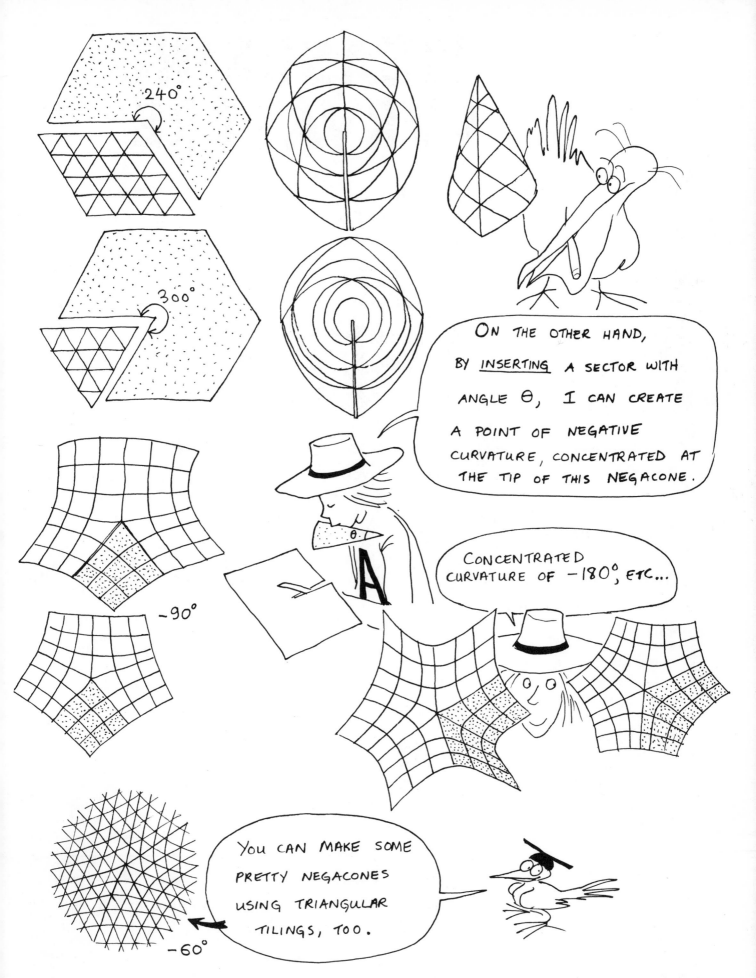

MEASURING CURVATURE

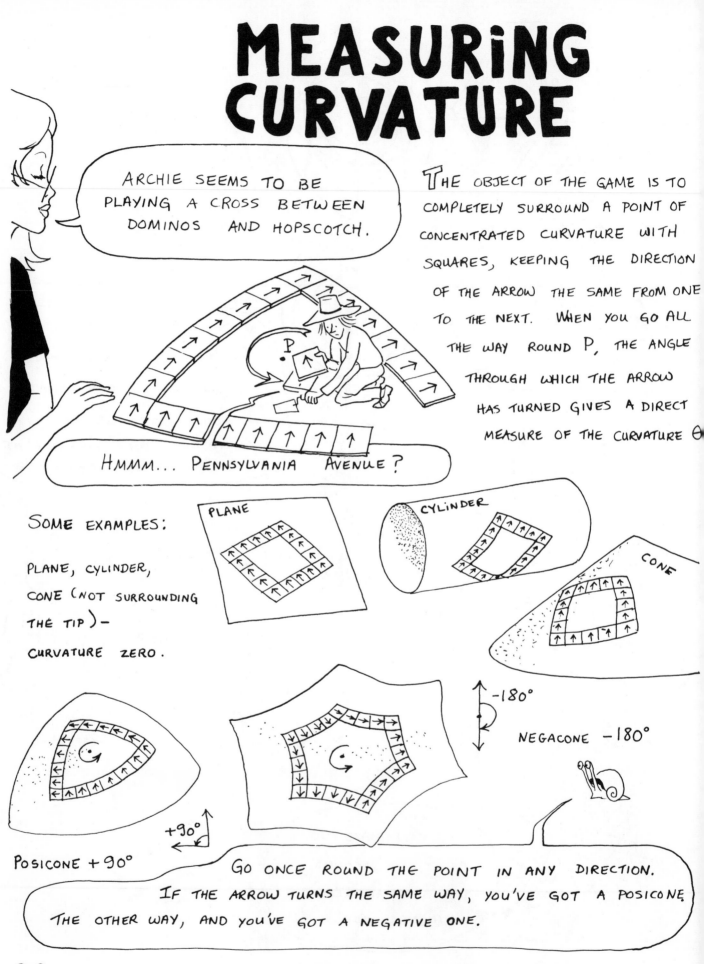

ARCHIE SEEMS TO BE PLAYING A CROSS BETWEEN DOMINOS AND HOPSCOTCH.

THE OBJECT OF THE GAME IS TO COMPLETELY SURROUND A POINT OF CONCENTRATED CURVATURE WITH SQUARES, KEEPING THE DIRECTION OF THE ARROW THE SAME FROM ONE TO THE NEXT. WHEN YOU GO ALL THE WAY ROUND P, THE ANGLE THROUGH WHICH THE ARROW HAS TURNED GIVES A DIRECT MEASURE OF THE CURVATURE θ

HMMM... PENNSYLVANIA AVENUE?

SOME EXAMPLES:

PLANE, CYLINDER, CONE (NOT SURROUNDING THE TIP)— CURVATURE ZERO.

PLANE

CYLINDER

CONE

−180°

NEGACONE −180°

POSICONE +90°

+90°

GO ONCE ROUND THE POINT IN ANY DIRECTION. IF THE ARROW TURNS THE SAME WAY, YOU'VE GOT A POSICONE, THE OTHER WAY, AND YOU'VE GOT A NEGATIVE ONE.

22

I'LL MAKE SOME NEARLY FLAT POSICONES, EACH WITH A VERY SMALL ANGLE θ.

ATOMS OF CURVATURE, SO TO SPEAK.

THEN I'LL GLUE THEM TOGETHER.

GLUE

I GET A SURFACE ON WHICH I CAN DRAW TRIANGLES MADE FROM STICKY-TAPE GEODESICS.

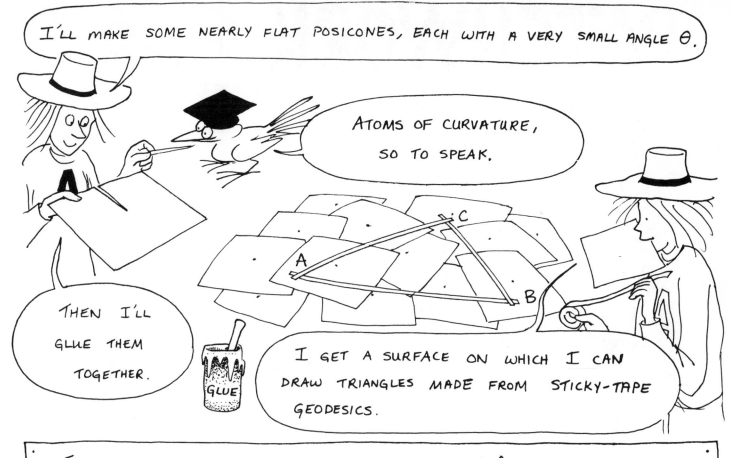

THE ANGLE-SUM OF A TRIANGLE EXCEEDS 180° BY AN AMOUNT EQUAL TO THE SUM OF THE ANGLES OF THE ELEMENTARY CONES WHOSE PEAKS ARE CONTAINED IN THE TRIANGLE.

The Boss

A CURVED SURFACE, IN THE USUAL SENSE OF THE PHRASE, CAN BE THOUGHT OF AS A VERY LARGE NUMBER OF TINY MICROCONES, GLUED TOGETHER.

YOU CAN ALSO JOIN TOGETHER NEGACONES; OR A MIXTURE OF POSICONES AND NEGACONES. IN THAT CASE, THE ANGLE-SUM OF A TRIANGLE WILL BE 180°, PLUS THE TOTAL AMOUNT OF CURVATURE INSIDE IT, COUNTED ALGEBRAICALLY (PLUS FOR POSICONES AND MINUS FOR NEGACONES).

23

PATCHWORK

SOPHIE: WHAT WILL I GET IF I ASSEMBLE A LOT OF NEGACONES?

FOR EXAMPLE, NEGACONES WITH $\theta = -180°$. THEIR BOUNDARY IS A HEXAGON WITH SIX RIGHT ANGLES.

SO YOU CAN JOIN THEM UP, FOUR AT A TIME.

BY PUTTING TWENTY OF THEM TOGETHER, YOU GET THIS PIECE OF A SURFACE OF NEGATIVE CURVATURE, ARRANGED LIKE THE TWENTY CORNERS OF A **DODECAHEDRON**. (*)

(*) FROM THE GREEK: DODEKA = TWELVE   'EDRON = SIDE

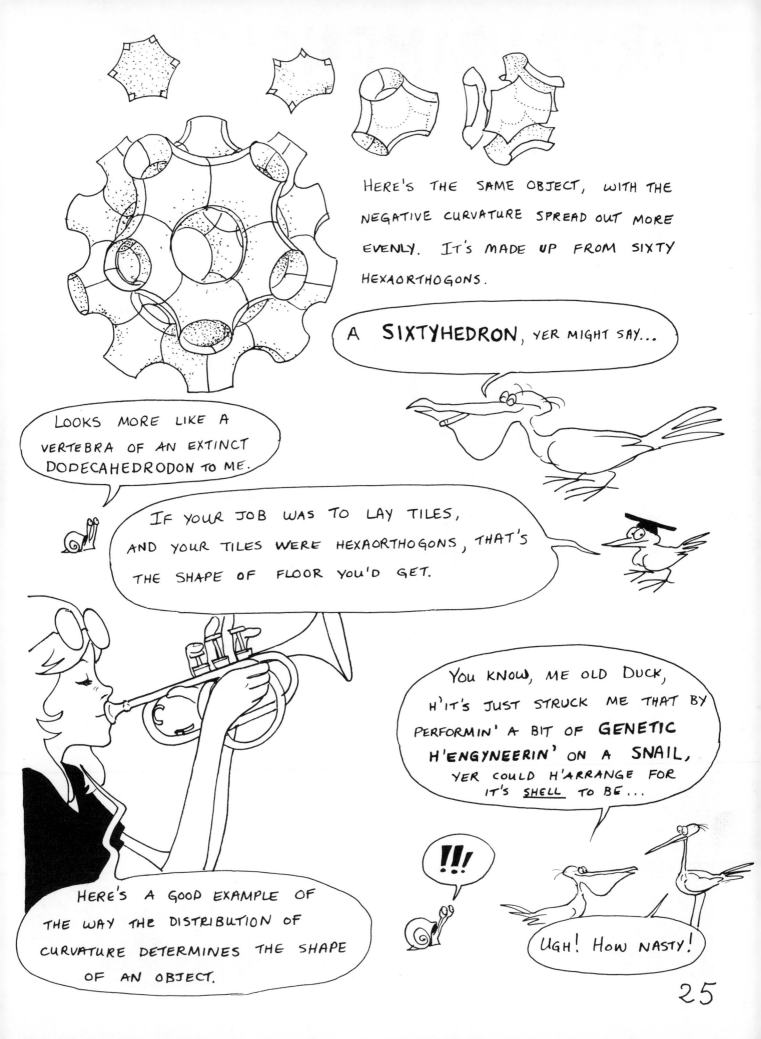

HERE'S THE SAME OBJECT, WITH THE NEGATIVE CURVATURE SPREAD OUT MORE EVENLY. IT'S MADE UP FROM SIXTY HEXAORTHOGONS.

A **SIXTYHEDRON**, YER MIGHT SAY...

LOOKS MORE LIKE A VERTEBRA OF AN EXTINCT DODECAHEDRODON TO ME.

IF YOUR JOB WAS TO LAY TILES, AND YOUR TILES WERE HEXAORTHOGONS, THAT'S THE SHAPE OF FLOOR YOU'D GET.

YOU KNOW, ME OLD DUCK, H'IT'S JUST STRUCK ME THAT BY PERFORMIN' A BIT OF **GENETIC H'ENGYNEERIN'** ON A **SNAIL**, YER COULD H'ARRANGE FOR IT'S <u>SHELL</u> TO BE...

!!!

HERE'S A GOOD EXAMPLE OF THE WAY THE DISTRIBUTION OF CURVATURE DETERMINES THE SHAPE OF AN OBJECT.

UGH! HOW NASTY!

THREE DIMENSIONS

SOPHIE, IS THERE ANY WAY TO <u>SEE</u> CURVATURE IN OUR USUAL SPACE OF <u>THREE</u> DIMENSIONS?

IT'S DIFFICULT, BECAUSE YOU'RE LIVING IN IT.

ONE WAY TO PICTURE THE CURVATURE OF A SURFACE IS TO PROJECT ITS GEODESICS ON TO A PLANE.

THIS 'BUMP' CORRESPONDS TO A CONCENTRATION OF POSITIVE CURVATURE, SURROUNDED BY A HALO OF NEGATIVE CURVATURE. IT'S AS PLAIN AS THE - ER - BEAK ON YOUR FACE, LENNY.

NOW, TAKE A LOOK AT THIS CUBE, ALL TIED UP WITH STRING.

I'LL SLIDE THE STRING SIDEWAYS, LIKE THIS.

BY FITTING TOGETHER
EIGHT OF THESE CUBES,
WE GET THE PROJECTION
INTO THREE-DIMENSIONAL EUCLIDEAN
SPACE (HAVING ZERO CURVATURE) OF THE GEODESICS IN
A PIECE OF A THREE-DIMENSIONAL SPACE, IN WHICH A
REGION OF POSITIVE CURVATURE IS SURROUNDED BY A
HALO OF NEGATIVE CURVATURE. A THREE-DIMENSIONAL BUMP!

IF YOU THINK OF THESE GEODESICS AS THE **TRAJECTORIES** OF A
MOVING PARTICLE, IT APPEARS TO UNDERGO FIRST A REPULSION, THEN AN
ATTRACTION, AND THEN A REPULSION AGAIN.

27

By sliding the strings like this, and joining up a large number of cubes, you can produce an image of a world populated by regions of both positive and negative curvature:

If you look at it closely you'll see it can also be built up by deforming the usual **CUBES** of Euclidean three-dimensional space.

It's very curious **THAT** you can pile up all these weird cubes and still fill up the space.

PROJECTIONS

LET ME CHECK I'VE GOT ALL THIS STRAIGHT, MR. ALBERT. YOU'RE SAYING THAT BENDS IN TRAJECTORIES, CAUSED BY FORCES, ARE REALLY JUST AN EFFECT OF THE PROJECTION, INTO OUR USUAL WORLD, OF A GEODESIC TRAJECTORY ON SOME OTHER SURFACE.

MORE RUDDY METAFIZZICKS!

NO, JUST GEOMETRY.

I GIF' YOU AN EXAMPLE. IMACHIN' YOURSELF TO BE IN A SPACE CAPSULE, IN ORBIT AROUND DER EARTH.

CRIKEY! WE'VE GONE WEIGHTLESS!

OH 'ECK!

¡IW

NOW WE CAN PLAY A RATHER UNUSUAL KIND OF BILLIARDS.

I didn't mean it, honest!

MASS AND MATTER

Are you saying that the sun is a... cone?

S

EARTH

MERCURY

MERCURY

EARTH

S

Well, we know it bends light rays from Mercury.

S'

WE USUALLY THINK OF SPACE NEAR THE SUN AS BEING **FLAT**. BUT IN FACT, BECAUSE OF ITS LARGE MASS, THIS STAR REPRESENTS A CERTAIN AMOUNT OF CURVATURE. BUT BECAUSE THE SUN'S MASS ISN'T CONCENTRATED AT A POINT, WE'LL THINK OF THIS REGION OF SPACE AS A SMOOTHED-OUT CONE.

I_1 E

STAR

MASSIVE OBJECT

I_2

OBSERVER

VERY MASSIVE OBJECTS CAN CURVE SPACE TO SUCH AN EXTENT THAT AN OBSERVER CAN SEE **TWO** IMAGES I_1 AND I_2 OF THE SAME STAR E. THIS EFFECT, KNOWN AS A **GRAVITATIONAL LENS**, HAS RECENTLY BEEN OBSERVED IN LIGHT FROM QUASARS.

WOT ABAHT **NEGACONES**, SMART ALECK?

THOSE CONJURE UP THE IDEA OF "NEGATIVE MASS," PRODUCING A REPULSIVE FORCE. A UNIVERSE FULL OF NEGATIVE MASSES WOULD BE VERY PECULIAR. INSTEAD OF GALAXIES, THERE WOULD BE LOTS OF BUBBLES — ENORMOUS VOIDS. IN FACT, THE MASS OF THE GALAXIES SEEMS TO BE DISTRIBUTED LIKE THIS, FORMING A STRANGE CELLULAR TISSUE. EACH CELL IS ABOUT 200 MILLION LIGHT=YEARS ACROSS.

PERHAPS GRAVITATIONAL FORCES BECOME REPULSIVE AT A VERY LARGE DISTANCE.

POLYHEDRA

Now, Archie: Remember that you can produce geodesics on a surface using sticky tape? What happens if you BEND the surface?

If you bend this cone ($\theta = 90°$) the geodesics don't change. (The sticky tape just bends with the surface.) In fact you can fold it to fit perfectly over the corner of a cube.

Similarly, you can make three folds in this cone ($\theta = 180°$) so that it fits over the corner of a regular tetrahedron.

SPACE MUST BE OPEN OR CLOSED

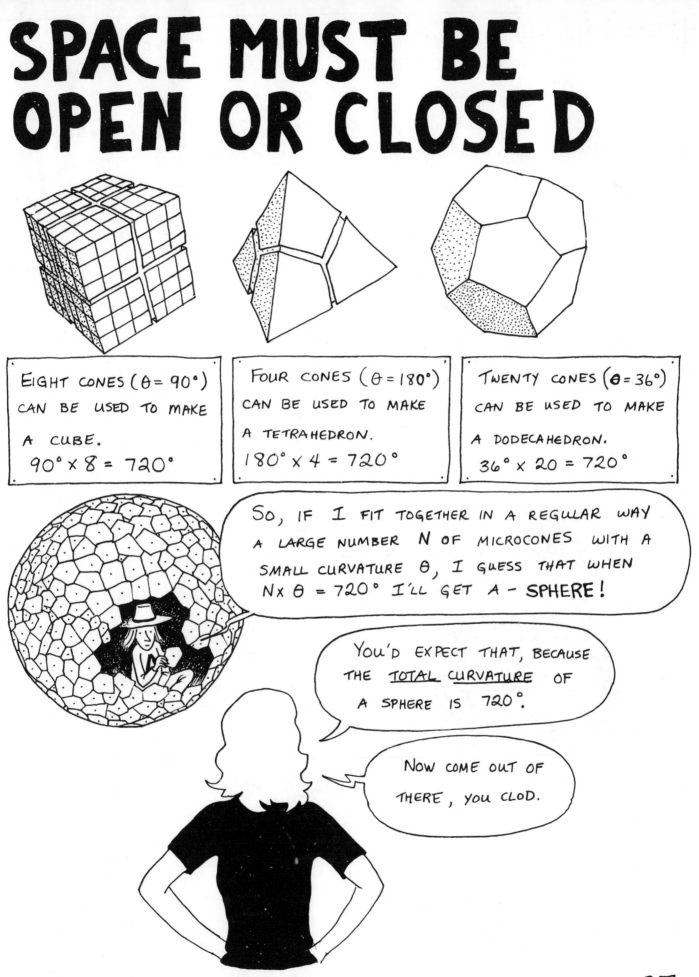

EIGHT CONES ($\theta = 90°$) CAN BE USED TO MAKE A CUBE.
$90° \times 8 = 720°$

FOUR CONES ($\theta = 180°$) CAN BE USED TO MAKE A TETRAHEDRON.
$180° \times 4 = 720°$

TWENTY CONES ($\theta = 36°$) CAN BE USED TO MAKE A DODECAHEDRON.
$36° \times 20 = 720°$

SO, IF I FIT TOGETHER IN A REGULAR WAY A LARGE NUMBER N OF MICROCONES WITH A SMALL CURVATURE θ, I GUESS THAT WHEN $N \times \theta = 720°$ I'LL GET A — SPHERE!

YOU'D EXPECT THAT, BECAUSE THE <u>TOTAL</u> CURVATURE OF A SPHERE IS 720°.

NOW COME OUT OF THERE, YOU CLOD.

On a sphere, the curvature is uniformly distributed. So the sum of the angles of a triangle drawn on a sphere is equal to $180° + 720° \times \frac{s}{S}$ where s is the area of the triangle and S the area of the sphere. The second term $720° \times \frac{s}{S}$ represents the **AMOUNT OF CURVATURE** contained in the triangle. (✱)

The Boss

For example, this triangle takes up one eighth of the surface of a sphere, and:

$$\hat{A} + \hat{B} + \hat{C} = 180° + \frac{720°}{8} = 270°$$

which is correct since all three angles are 90.°

STAGGERIN'!

In der same cheneral line of ideas, if der minimum density in our three-dimensional space (dat is, der curfature per unit volume) is more dan 10^{-29} gm/cm^3, den space closes up on itself like a sphere.

Mr. Albert, tell me, what's the total curvature of a **TORUS**?

Simple, Archibald. All you haf' to do is think of it <u>dis</u> way: eight posicones ($\theta = +90°$) and eight negacones ($\theta = -90°$)

(✱) A theorem of Gauss

A TORUS WITH N HOLES, A FOUGASSE(*), WILL HAVE A TOTAL CURVATURE OF $-4\pi(N-1)$. YOU LOSE 4π FOR EACH HOLE.

(*) A FOUGASSE IS A SORT OF LOAF MADE IN THE SOUTH OF FRANCE, WHERE THE AUTHOR LIVES.

40

41

ANYONE WHO THOUGHT HE WAS LIVING IN A **PLANAR** WORLD WOULD THINK OF THE TRAJECTORIES LIKE THIS.

HORIZON

YOU CAN MAKE YOUR OWN BLACK HOLE USING A PLANE WITH A HOLE IN IT (①), SIX TRUNCATED CONES (JOINED EDGE TO EDGE) AND A CYLINDER (⑧).

PLANE

① ② ③ ④ ⑤ ⑥ ⑦ ⑧

CYLINDER

VARIATIONS

42

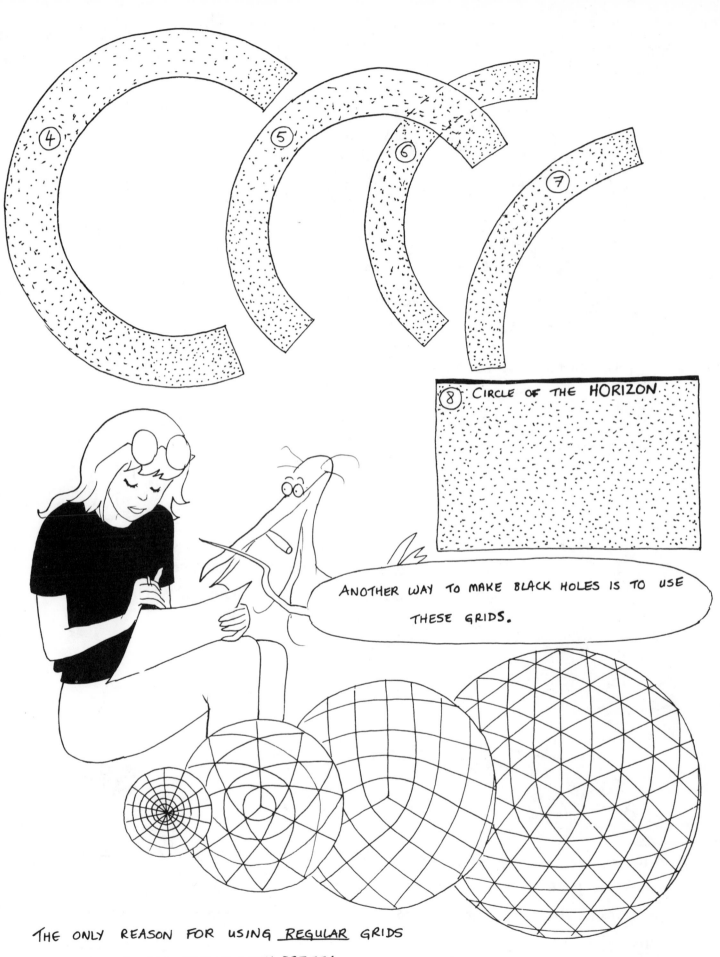

CIRCLE OF THE HORIZON

ANOTHER WAY TO MAKE BLACK HOLES IS TO USE THESE GRIDS.

THE ONLY REASON FOR USING <u>REGULAR</u> GRIDS IS TO MAKE THE RESULT LOOK PRETTY.

RULES OF THE GAME: YOU MUST DRAW LINES THAT CUT EACH GRID AT A FIXED ANGLE, WHILE MAINTAINING CONSISTENCY AND CONTINUITY AT EACH BOUNDARY CIRCLE WHERE THE GRIDS JOIN UP. THE CLOSER YOU APPROACH THE BLACK HOLE, THE STRONGER ITS ATTRACTION WILL SEEM. WITHIN THE HORIZON CIRCLE THE TRAJECTORY WILL ROLL UP INTO A SPIRAL. NOTE THAT THE CENTRAL GRID, WHICH IS POLE-SHAPED, CAN BE OBTAINED FROM A GRID OF GEODESICS ON THE CYLINDER, VIEWED IN PERSPECTIVE.

'ANG ON THERE! SEEMS TER ME THERE'S SUMFINK A BIT <u>COCKEYED</u> ABAHT THIS 'OLE SET-UP!

YER'VE REPLACED MASSES BY CURVYTURES AND TRAJECTORIES BY BLINKIN' GEO-DEESICKS. BUT WOTCHA GONNA DO ABAHT THE H'INITIAL VELOCIPEDE?

THE TRAJECTORY FOLLOWED BY AN OBJECT WITHIN THE FIELD OF FORCE GENERATED BY ONE OR SEVERAL MASSE. DEPENDS ON ITS <u>INITIAL VELOCITY</u> V_0.

FOR EXAMPLE: CANNONBALLS IN EARTH'S GRAVITATIONAL FIELD.

44

DOES THAT MEAN THAT ALL THE DRAWINGS SO FAR CORRESPOND TO JUST ONE PARTICULAR VALUE OF THE INITIAL VELOCITY V_0?

THE ABYSS

THINK OF A WORLD BUILT LIKE AN ONION, IN CONCENTRIC LAYERS. (*)

COSMIC PARK

TO EACH LAYER THERE CORRESPONDS A MAGNITUDE V OF THE VELOCITY. THE FASTER YOU GO, THE DEEPER YOU GO.

AT THE SPEED OF LIGHT, YOU REACH THE MIDDLE OF THE ONION.

(*) THIS MODEL HAS BEEN INTRODUCED IN **EVERYTHING IS RELATIVE** (SAME SERIES) UNDER THE NAME <u>COSMIC PARK</u>.

IF THERE ARE NO FORCES, THEN THE SPEED OF THE OBJECT DOESN'T CHANGE. SO IT STAYS ON A **SPHERE**, ALWAYS THE SAME DISTANCE FROM THE CENTER OF THE ONION. IT FOLLOWS A GEODESIC, THAT IS, A **GREAT CIRCLE**, ON THIS SPHERE.

THIS WILL DO THE TRICK!

WHEN MR. ALBERT HIT IT WITH HIS HAMMER, THIS IS WHAT HAPPENED. YOU CAN SEE THAT THE EFFECT GETS LESS NEARER THE CENTER.

HERE IS A **DENT** (OR A **BUMP**, IT MAKES NO DIFFERENCE). THE CONTOUR LEVELS (WHICH ARE **NOT** GEODESICS!) HAVE BEEN DRAWN, ALONG WITH ONE SELECTED GEODESIC.

46

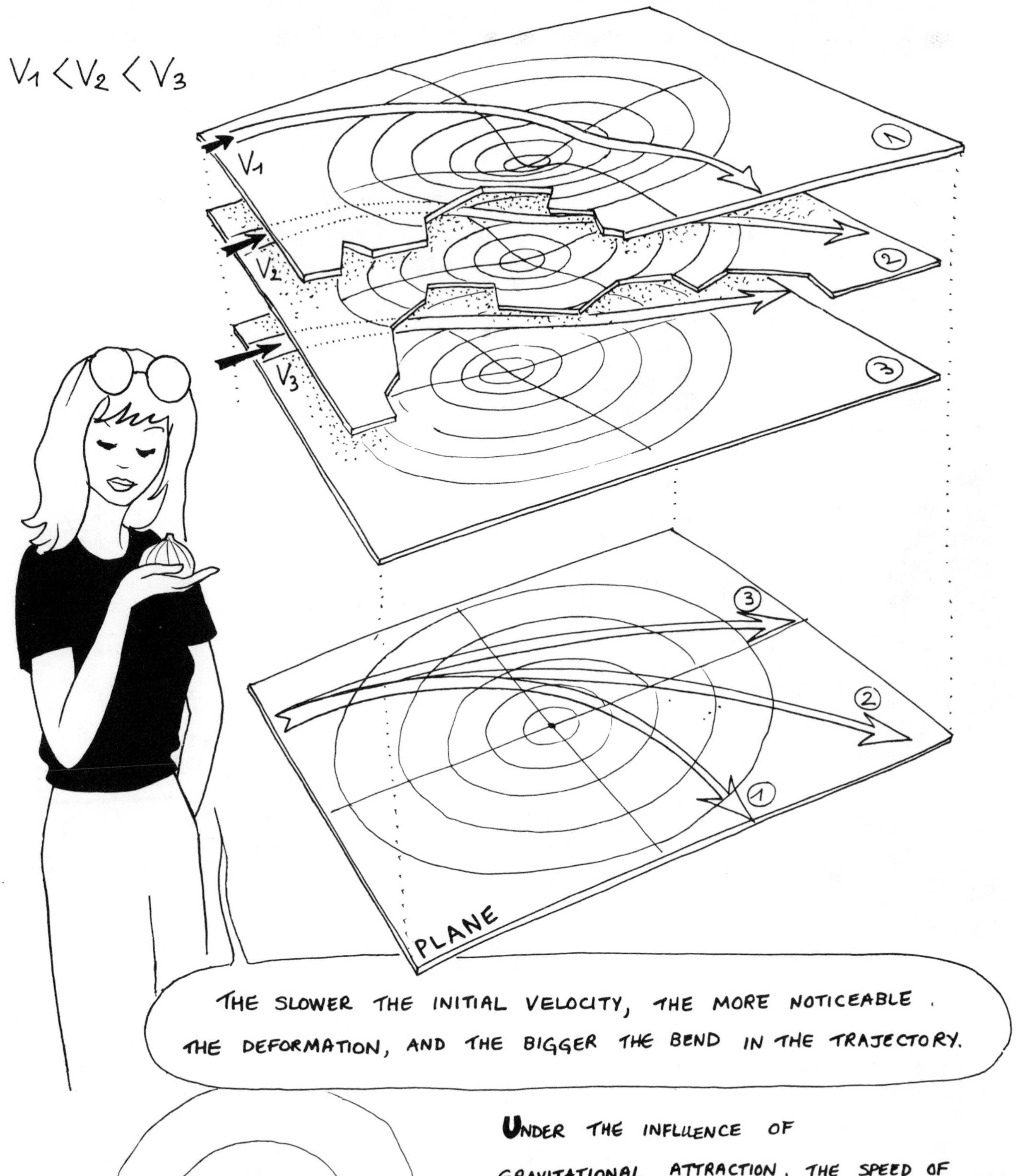

$V_1 < V_2 < V_3$

V_1

V_2

V_3

① ② ③

③

②

①

PLANE

THE SLOWER THE INITIAL VELOCITY, THE MORE NOTICEABLE
THE DEFORMATION, AND THE BIGGER THE BEND IN THE TRAJECTORY.

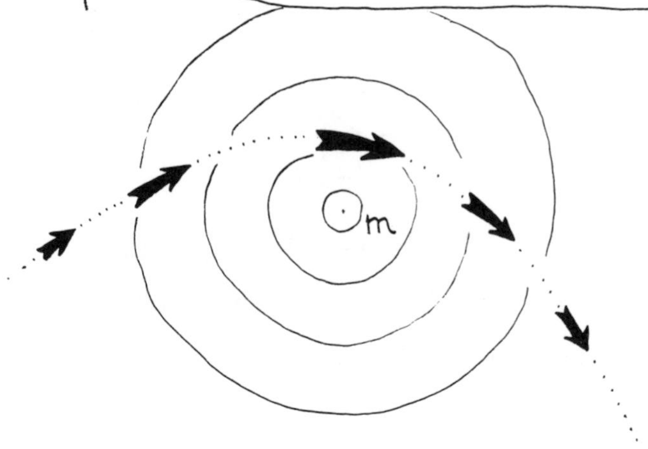

O_m

UNDER THE INFLUENCE OF
GRAVITATIONAL ATTRACTION, THE SPEED OF
AN OBJECT FIRST INCREASES, THEN
DECREASES. IT IS GREATEST WHEN
THE DISTANCE BETWEEN THE OBJECT AND
THE ATTRACTING MASS IS SMALLEST.
ASTRONOMERS CALL THIS POSITION
PERIHELION.

47

SINCE THE PRESSURE P_R IS GREATER THAN P_E, THE CHRONOL FLOWS OUT AND THE CHRONOMETER SHOWS THE TIME THAT HAS PASSED.

THE DEEPER YOU DESCEND INTO THE CHRONOL, THE MORE THE PRESSURE P_E INCREASES. SINCE THE RATE OF FLOW IS PROPORTIONAL TO $(P_R - P_E)$, THE PRESSURE-DIFFERENCE, TIME FLOWS MORE SLOWLY AT GREATER DEPTHS.

THE DEPTH IS THE SPEED. SO THE FASTER YOU GO, THE SLOWER TIME PASSES. (*)

AND AT THE SPEED OF LIGHT, P_E IS EXACTLY EQUAL TO P_R, AND TIME GRINDS TO A HALT.

AND YOU CAN'T TRAVEL FASTER THAN LIGHT, BECAUSE YOU CAN'T GO ANY DEEPER THAN THE CENTER OF COSMIC PARK.

(*) SEE EVERYTHING IS RELATIVE, SAME SERIES.

50

THE OUTSIDE SURFACE OF COSMIC PARK CORRESPONDS TO NO MOTION AT ALL: THE **REST STATE**.

WHEN YOU STAY STILL YOU AGE FASTEST!

REST STATE

A VERY MASSIVE BODY PRODUCES A LARGE AMOUNT OF CURVATURE IN SPACE-TIME. THIS MEANS THAT ANY NEARBY OBJECT, EVEN ONE AT REST, IS IMMERSED IN **CHRONOL** AT A HIGHER PRESSURE. SO, FOR IT, TIME FLOWS MORE SLOWLY THAN IT WOULD FOR AN OBJECT AT REST, BUT FAR FROM ANY MASS. THIS SLOWING DOWN OF TIME HAPPENS, FOR INSTANCE, NEAR A SUPERDENSE OBJECT SUCH AS A **NEUTRON STAR**.

WOT 'APPENS TO A BLOKE 'OO SCARPERS OUT OF 'IS CHRONOSCAPHE?

HE PROBABLY GETS A SUDDEN ATTACK OF OLD AGE.

PR

CHRONOL

CHRONOMETER

AND WHEN ALL THE CHRONOL RUNS OUT, IS THAT... DEATH?

51

COMMUNICATION

WELL, HERE WE ARE INSIDE OUR CHRONOSCAPHES. HOW CAN WE COMMUNICATE WITH EACH OTHER?

BY USING **PHOTONS**.

PHOTONS — TINY QUANTITIES OF LIGHT — BEHAVE JUST LIKE A SEARCHLIGHT BEAM, SWEEPING ACROSS ALL THE LAYERS OF COSMIC PARK AT A CONSTANT ANGULAR VELOCITY.

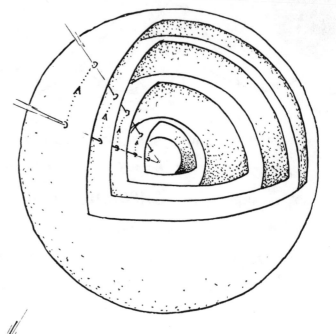

REST STATE

SPEED V_A

SPEED V_B

$V_B > V_A$

A

B

AN OBJECT A, TRAVELING AT A SPEED V_A, CAN TRIGGER OFF ONE OF THESE SEARCHLIGHT BEAMS IN THE DIRECTION OF AN OBJECT B, MOVING AT A SPEED V_B.

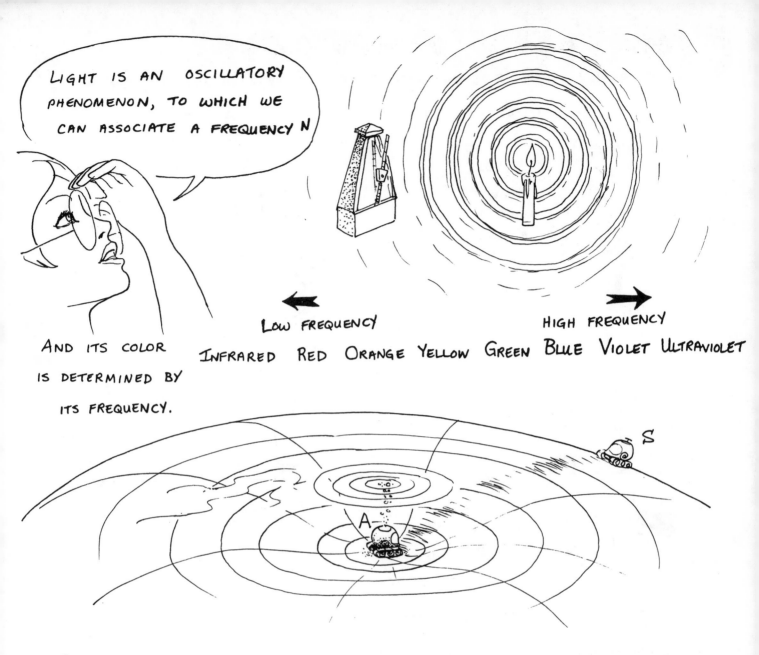

LIGHT IS AN OSCILLATORY PHENOMENON, TO WHICH WE CAN ASSOCIATE A FREQUENCY N

AND ITS COLOR IS DETERMINED BY ITS FREQUENCY.

← LOW FREQUENCY   HIGH FREQUENCY →

INFRARED RED ORANGE YELLOW GREEN BLUE VIOLET ULTRAVIOLET

THE FREQUENCIES OF THE PHOTONS EMITTED OR RECEIVED WILL BE MEASURED RELATIVE TO THE FLOW-RATE OF TIME IN THE CHRONOSCAPHE OF THE EMITTER OR RECEIVER. IN CHRONOSCAPHE A, ARCHIE SENDS OUT BLUE LIGHT. HE HAPPENS TO BE IN A REGION OF SPACE THAT IS HIGHLY CURVED — FOR EXAMPLE, HE MAY BE NEAR A NEUTRON STAR OF ENORMOUS MASS.

SOPHIE, IN CHRONOSCAPHE S, RECEIVES THIS LIGHT. SHE IS A LONG WAY FROM THE SUPERDENSE OBJECT. SO HER TIME FLOWS FASTER, AND SHE MEASURES A LOWER FREQUENCY. TO HER, THE COLOR OF THE LIGHT SEEMS TO HAVE SHIFTED TOWARDS RED.

ARCHIE IS STANDING ON A NEUTRON STAR. (WE HAVE TEMPORARILY SUSPENDED THE EFFECTS OF GRAVITY ON HIS BODY, SINCE THAT WOULD INSTANTLY SPREAD HIM OUT FLATTER THAN A PANCAKE.)

SECOND ENCOUNTER WITH A BLACK HOLE

I WANT TO EXPLORE COSMIC PARK SOME MORE.

JA, JA. UND LENNY UND I VILL COME TOO! HAF' A NICE GEODESIC!

YES, AND I'M IN VOICE CONTACT WITH THEM, BY RADIO. (*)

I SEE LENNY AND MR. ALBERT OVER THERE.

WOOPS, WHAT'S THAT THING IN THE DISTANCE?

LOOKS LIKE A TRUMPET — OR A TORNADO.

(*) RADIO WAVES ARE SIMILAR TO LIGHT WAVES. THEY HAVE THE SAME SPEED OF PROPAGATION C, BUT LOWER FREQUENCY.

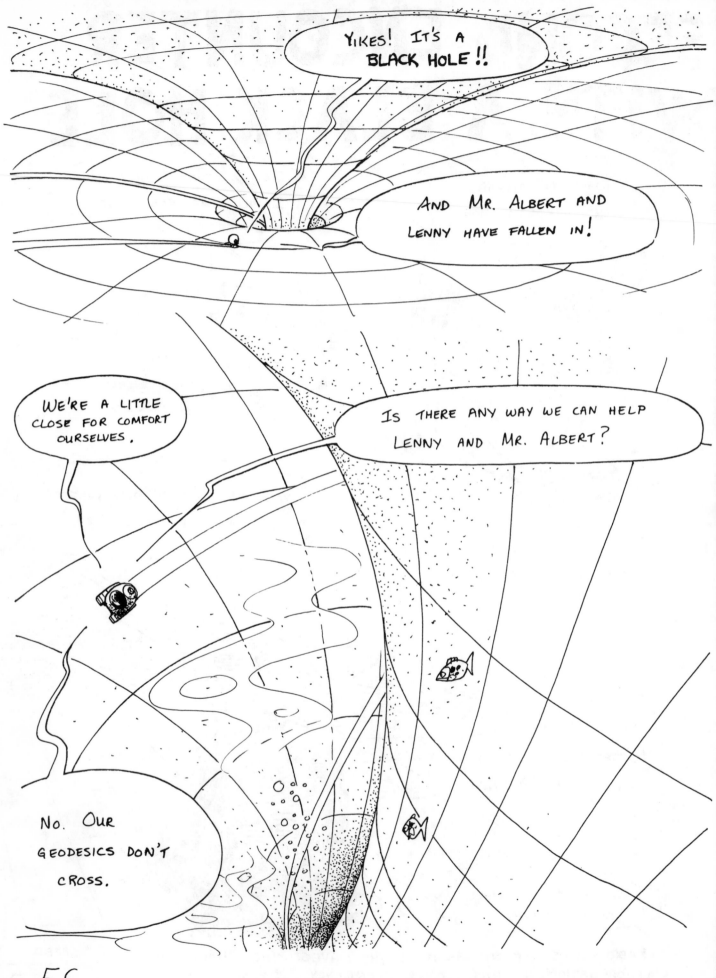

56

57

A MATTER OF TIME

THE DEEPER MR. ALBERT AND LENNY SINK INTO THE CHRONOL, THE MORE THE OUTSIDE PRESSURE P_e INCREASES, THE SLOWER THE CLEPSYDRA RUNS OUT OF CHRONOL, AND THE SLOWER TIME FLOWS IN THEIR CHRONOSCAPHE.

WHEN THEY GET DOWN TO THE BOTTOM OF THINGS, AT THE SPEED OF LIGHT, THEIR WATER-CLOCK HAS LOST ONLY A LIMITED AMOUNT OF CHRONOL, WHICH MEANS THAT THEY REACH THE BOTTOM IN A <u>FINITE</u> TIME, ACCORDING TO THE TIME FLOWING IN THEIR OWN CHRONOSCAPHE. BUT IF SOPHIE, ARCHIE, MAX, AND TIRESIAS COULD CONTINUE TO TRACK THEIR DESCENT, TO THEM IT WOULD SEEM INTERMINABLE. THE LIGHT EMITTED BY THE CHRONOSCAPHE WOULD DROP DEEP INTO THE INFRARED, BELOW THE RANGE OF VISIBLE LIGHT, WHILE THE RADIO MESSAGE WOULD SOUND LOWER AND LOWER AND SLOWER AND SLOWER.

IT REMINDS ME OF THE PARADOX OF ACHILLES AND THE SNAIL. ACHILLES TRIES TO CATCH THE SNAIL, BY REPEATEDLY HALVING THE DISTANCE BETWEEN THEM. YOU'D THINK IT WOULD GO ON FOREVER, BUT THE STEPS ADD UP TO A <u>FINITE</u> TOTAL TIME.

HERE IS A PICTURE OF A BLACK HOLE, ACCORDING TO THE COSMIC PARK MODEL. THE SPIKE HAS PENETRATED ALL THE WAY TO THE CENTER OF SPACE-TIME, WHERE THE SPEED IS THAT OF LIGHT. ALL THE LAYERS HAVE BECOME TANGENT TO A CONE WITH VERTEX SEMI-ANGLE α.

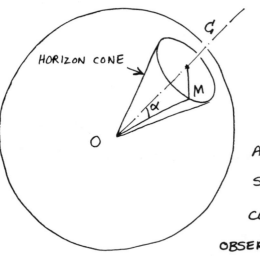

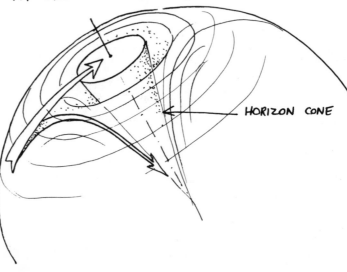

IN THIS MODEL, DISTANCE IS ACTUALLY AN ANGLE BETWEEN TWO RADIAL VECTORS, SUCH AS $\overrightarrow{OM}$ AND $\overrightarrow{OC}$. FROM THE DIAGRAM ABOVE YOU CAN SEE THAT NOTHING CAN PENETRATE INSIDE THIS CONE WITH SEMI-ANGLE α. IMAGINE AN OBSERVER IN A REST STATE AT THE SURFACE OF THE CHRONOL, WHO DOESN'T REALIZE SPACE-TIME IS CURVED. TO HIM, THE FRONTIER OF THE BLACK HOLE - THE **EVENT HORIZON** - LOOKS LIKE A **CIRCLE**, WHICH IS REACHED AT THE SPEED OF LIGHT.

REST STATE

OH LOOK, THIS IS WHERE WE CAME IN — BACK AT CHRONOSCAPHE #3, WHICH HASN'T MOVED.

OUR LITTLE EXCURSION AROUND THE BLACK HOLE HAS SLOWED DOWN OUR AGING PROCESSES. IF ONE OF US HAD STAYED AT REST IN THE THIRD CHRONOSCAPHE, HE WOULD HAVE HAD TO WAIT HUNDREDS OR MAYBE MILLIONS OF YEARS FOR OUR RETURN.

WHERE DO BLACK HOLES LEAD TO?

NOBODY KNOWS. ACCORDING TO THE THEORISTS, AN ANTI-BLACK HOLE COULD EXIST.

THAT WOULD BE A REGION THAT NOBODY COULD ENTER. ALL YOU COULD DO WOULD BE TO COME OUT OF IT! WOW!

A WHITE FOUNTAIN

60

IN THE COSMIC PARK MODEL, HERE'S A WAY YOU COULD JOIN UP A BLACK HOLE/WHITE FOUNTAIN PAIR.

THE WHITE FOUNTAIN IS EXACTLY THE SAME, EXCEPT THAT ITS GEODESICS HAVE THEIR ORIENTATION REVERSED.

BUT WOT'S H'INSIDE A BLACK 'OLE, OVER THE BLINKIN' 'ORIZON? IS IT JUST A LOAD OF... NUFFIN'?

YOU MEAN THAT THE INTERIOR OF A BLACK HOLE IS PURE NONEXISTENCE?

NO, NO! THE "INTERIOR" OF THE BLACK HOLE IS JUST THE EXTERIOR OF ITS ASSOCIATED WHITE FOUNTAIN.

THE ALERT READER WILL HAVE NOTICED THAT IN THIS MODEL THE BLACK HOLE/WHITE FOUNTAIN PAIR GIVES ALL THE LAYERS OF COSMIC PARK THE STRUCTURE OF A NONORIENTABLE SURFACE, WITH ONLY ONE SIDE. PASSAGE THROUGH THE HOLE SENDS OBJECTS INTO THEIR MIRROR IMAGES. FOR EXAMPLE, R COMES OUT AS Я.

AS CLEAR AS MUD

62

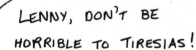

EPILOGUE

THE
END

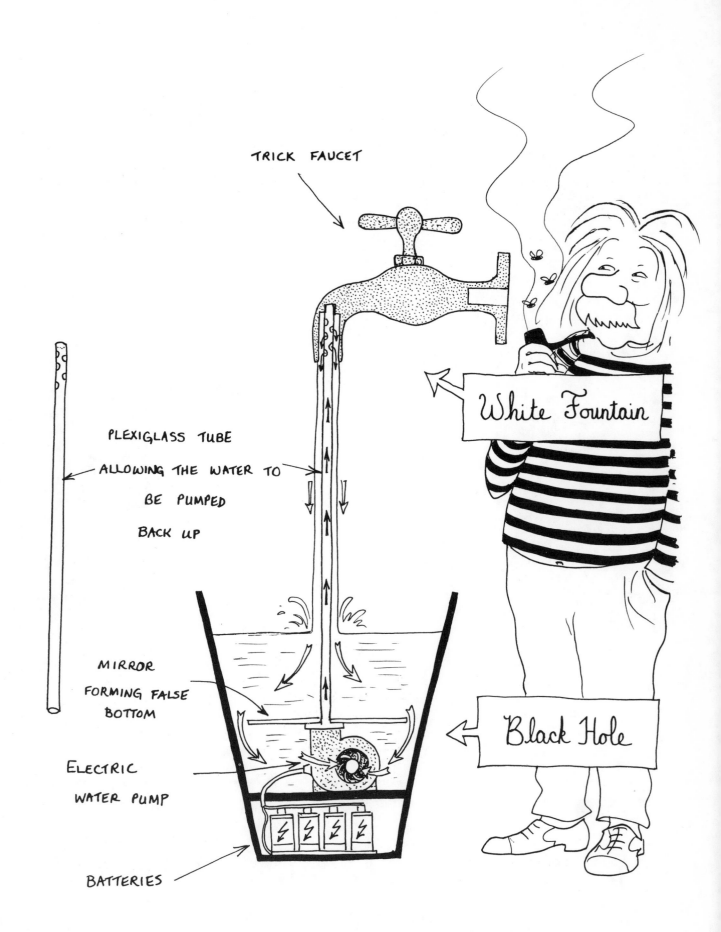